DISCARDED

Aboriginal Legends of Canada

Huron

Megan Cuthbert

Weigl

Published by Weigl Educational Publishers Limited
6325 10th Street SE
Calgary, Alberta T2H 2Z9

Website: www.weigl.ca

Library and Archives Canada Cataloguing in Publication available upon request.
Fax 403-233-7769 for the attention of the Publishing Records Department.

ISBN 978-1-77071-554-7 (hardcover)
ISBN 978-1-77071-555-4 (softcover)
ISBN 978-1-77071-556-1 (multi-user eBook)

Printed in the United States of America in North Mankato, Minnesota
1 2 3 4 5 6 7 8 9 0 17 16 15 14 13

072013
WEP130613

Senior Editor: Heather Kissock
Editor: Alexis Roumanis
Design: Mandy Christiansen
Illustrator: Martha Jablonski-Jones

Photo Credits
Weigl acknowledges Alamy and Getty Images as its primary image suppliers for this title.

We acknowledge the financial support of the Government of Canada through the Canada Book Fund for our publishing activities.

CONTENTS

Meet the Huron

The Huron are one of Canada's **Aboriginal** groups. They are sometimes called the Wendat as well. The Huron's **traditional** lands are found in Ontario and Quebec. Today, there are about 3,000 Huron. Most live in the village of Lorette, near Quebec City. Some also live in the United States.

Storytelling has long been an important part of Huron life. People would gather around campfires to listen to **elders** tell stories. While the stories were often told in an entertaining way, their main purpose was to teach. Some Huron stories present how their world came to be. There are also stories that teach lessons, explaining how a person's behaviour can affect his or her life.

Stories of Creation

The Huron use storytelling as a way to pass on their beliefs to younger people and also introduce Huron beliefs to others. One of the most important types of stories is the creation story. This **legend** explains how and why the world was formed and how humans and animals came to live there.

Females played an important role in Huron society. Women were in charge of the daily activities within their village. They cared for the children, made clothing and baskets, and cooked food.

The Huron creation story explains how Earth was made because of events that happened in the sky. The Huron believed that, in the beginning, there was only Sky World and the water and the creatures that lived within each. It was only when a woman fell from the sky that Earth began to form.

The Huron lived in an area with many lakes and rivers. Part of their diet included fish such as trout and sturgeon.

The Huron believed that all living things and objects had a spirit. The most powerful spirit was the sky spirit, who appeared to the Huron as the wind.

The Story of SKY MOTHER

In the beginning, the world was only water and only water animals lived in it. Then one day, a powerful woman fell from a torn place in the sky. Two birds came flying over to the falling woman. They flew under her, breaking her fall, and then called for the other animals to come help.

The animals knew that the woman would not survive in the water. She needed something solid to live on. They decided that they would try diving into the water to bring up dirt from the bottom of the ocean. Each animal took its turn at diving into the water. Most ran out of breath and were unsuccessful. Finally, a toad went down and was able to bring up some dirt in his mouth.

The woman took the dirt and spread it on a turtle's shell. This was the start of Earth. The land grew until it formed a country, and then another country, and eventually all the Earth. To this day, Turtle still holds up Earth.

Nature Stories

The Huron find deep **spiritual** meaning in the sky, land, and water that surround them. They use stories to explain the importance of nature in their daily lives. Several Huron stories explain events that occur in the **natural world**.

Rainbow's Punishment explains how the rainbow came to be. The story also stresses why it is important to keep nature in balance. The Huron believe that all living things have a role in the world. This is what keeps Earth in balance. When one living thing is no longer in the world, the rest of the world feels the impact.

Each animal in an ecosystem depends on other animals or plants to survive. Whatever happens to one plant or animal affects the whole community.

The Huron believe that, at one time, the rainbow was a bridge to the Sky World.

Rainbow's PUNISHMENT

One day, Deer decided he wanted to visit his sister in the Sky World. He asked Rainbow if she would build him a beautiful bridge to the sky. Rainbow built the bridge for Deer. When Deer went up to the Sky World, he decided not to return to the world below. Not long after Deer climbed the bridge, Bear went up to the Sky World to bring Deer back.

The other animals down below became worried. They had a meeting and asked Rainbow to explain why she built the bridge. Rainbow explained that she had built the bridge because Deer had asked her to. The animals decided that Rainbow had to be punished for the disappearance of Deer and Bear. They burned the bridge to the Sky World that Rainbow had built.

From that day on, Rainbow could only appear after a rain shower as an arc in the rays of the Sun. She could no longer reach the sky.

Life Lessons

One of the main reasons the Huron tell stories is to teach important life lessons. Many of their stories use characters and animals to explain how people should behave and what can happen if a person does not behave properly. The stories often include funny moments, but the lessons they teach are very serious.

Some Huron pass on stories or legends through embroidery. They sew designs and patterns onto clothing, belts, bags, and blankets. These designs often feature symbols and images from a popular Huron legend.

After Sky Mother fell from Sky World, she gave birth to two sons, Tijus-kaha and Tawis-karong. One of the brothers was good, while the other was evil. Through the actions of the good and bad sons, Huron storytellers can show what happens to people who behave well and to people who do not.

Tijus-kaha was known for creating animals that the Huron could use, such as the partridge. Tawis-karong created animals that caused problems for the Huron. The giant toad, for instance, drank all of Earth's water.

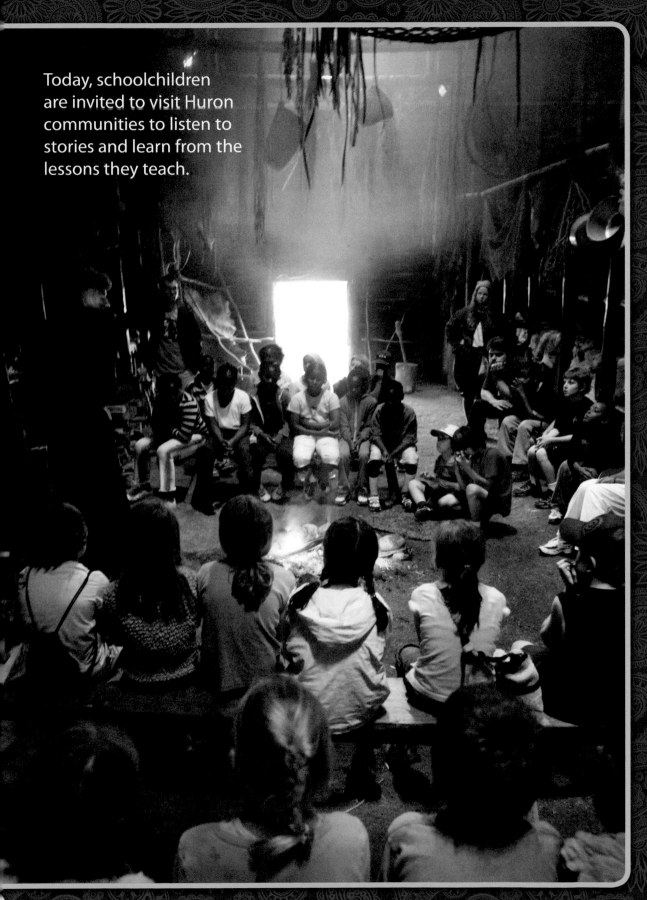

Today, schoolchildren are invited to visit Huron communities to listen to stories and learn from the lessons they teach.

BUZZARD'S COAT

Tijus-kaha went up to Sky World. While he was away, his wicked brother Tawis-karong stole the feathers of every bird.

The birds were upset. They looked ugly without their feathers and wanted them back. Buzzard offered to find the feather coats and bring them back. Singer volunteered to help his friend Buzzard.

The two birds flew to Tawis-karong's cave and found the feather coats. Buzzard wanted to see if he could look better in someone else's coat. He began to try on the many feather coats. Singer took a simple coat of black feathers to wear. As Buzzard was trying on a beautiful coat of many coloured feathers, Tawis-karong returned. Singer flew to Tawis-karong and started pecking at his head. Buzzard escaped, taking the bag of coats with him.

By the time Buzzard arrived home, Tijus-kaha had returned. He became angry when he learned that Buzzard had wasted time trying on other coats. When Singer flew in, Tijus-kaha was so pleased with him that he took the beautiful coat of feathers from Buzzard and gave it to Singer. He then took Singer's plain black coat and gave it to Buzzard.

Heroic Tales

Many Huron stories tell of people who display great bravery. These heroes act in remarkable ways to help others. Some of these people are quite ordinary. They have no special powers or skills. They just do what they think is right. In this way, they set an example for others to follow.

In *The First Garden*, an old man is rewarded for his kind behaviour and is given the seeds to create the first garden. At one time, gardening and farming provided much of the food in a Huron village. The Huron lived in an area that had fertile soil. Many different food plants, including corn, pumpkins, and sunflowers, could be grown there.

The Huron farmed in cycles. When strawberries were ripe, the Huron knew it was time to plant pumpkins and corn.

Sunflowers were valuable to the Huron because of their seeds. The seeds could be roasted and eaten, or ground into flour. Their oil could be used as a body lotion.

The FIRST GARDEN

An old man lived in a village with his wife and two daughters. One day, the man's wife and children went to the Land of the Little People, leaving the old man alone. Despite his sadness, the man went about the village doing good for the people.

One morning, the man saw a large flock of hawks fly over the village. A hawk with bright red wings fell to the ground.

The people of the village were scared. They had never seen a hawk so large. They ran away from it in fear.

The old man was brave and went to check on the hawk. A bright flame came from the sky and burned the hawk to ashes. In the ashes, the old man saw his eldest daughter. She explained that the Little People had sent her down to the village with seeds from the Tree of Light. She planted the seeds in the ashes around her, and a large field of corn began to grow. Soon, there were also squashes, pumpkins, and beans as well. The old man realized that his troubles had not been for nothing, and he was happy once more.

Activity

Grow Your Own Garden

The Huron were great farmers and gardeners. They used the plants they grew to make most of their food. Follow these instructions to grow your own vegetables.

You Will Need:

| vegetable seeds | soil | planter | water |

1. Add soil into the empty planter. Then, place a few seeds in the soil. Cover the seeds with more soil.

2. Add some water so that the soil is damp.

3. Put your plant in a sunny place. Water the plant every few days, and see if your plant can grow.

Further Research

Many books and websites provide information on Aboriginal legends. To learn more about this topic, borrow books from the library, or search the internet.

Books

Most libraries have computers that connect to a database for researching information. If you input a key word, you will be provided with a list of books in the library that contain information on that topic. Nonfiction books are arranged numerically, using their call number. Fiction books are organized alphabetically by the author's last name.

Websites

Learn more about the Huron at: www.collectionscanada.gc.ca/settlement/kids/021013-2111-e.html

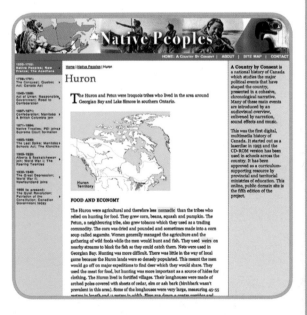

To learn how the Huron lived long ago, visit: www.canadahistoryproject.ca/1500/1500-06-huron.html

Key Words

Aboriginal: First Nations, Inuit, and Métis of Canada

elders: the wise people of a community

legend: a story that has been passed down from generation to generation

natural world: relating to things that have not been made by people

spiritual: of or related to sacred matters

traditional: related to established beliefs or practices

Index